T0052688

Ladders

Living
IN THE
MOUNTAINS
Communities We Live In

TALL MOUNTAINS,

"We made it!" exclaimed Jordan Romero as he stood on the peak of Vinson Massif, the highest mountain in Antarctica. Above him was a bright blue sky. Below him were rocky peaks and miles of snow. On December 24, 2011, Jordan had reached his **goal** to climb the highest mountain on every **continent**, or large landmass on Earth.

Jordan set this goal when he was only 10. He noticed a mural at school showing the highest mountain peaks, or **summits**, on the seven continents. Immediately Jordan thought, "I'd like to climb these mountains!" But there

∧ Climbing rope

< Jordan stands between his stepmom on the left and his dad on the right. They are at the top of Vinson Massif.

Big Goals

by Debbie Nevins
and Ann Wildman

was plenty he had to do before starting his climbs. Jordan and his dad had to get permission from each country to climb its highest peak. They needed to get the right climbing gear. And most importantly, Jordan had to train for these big climbs. He was already living an active, healthy life in the mountain community of Big Bear Lake, California. He was used to running and climbing in the mountains. But Jordan would have to do special training to meet such a big goal.

Vinson Massif is located in Antarctica. It was discovered in 1935.

The Seven Summits

With his dad to guide him, Jordan began hiking in the Sierra Nevada, a mountain range near his community, carrying a heavy backpack to build his strength. He also went running in the mountains near his home to learn to breathe at high **elevations**. Elevation is the height of a mountain peak above sea level, or the surface of the sea. At higher elevations, it is harder to

Follow along as Jordan and his team climb the "Seven Summits."

SUMMIT 4
Mount Aconcagua
(ah-kawng-KAH-gwah)
in South America
22,841 feet

JORDAN'S CLIMB
December 2007, age 11

This mountain's very strong winds tested Jordan's body and mind. Only Jordan, his dad, and his stepmom made it to the summit.

SUMMIT 3
Mount Elbrus
in Europe
18,510 feet

JORDAN'S CLIMB
July 2007, age 10

Jordan took the lead on this climb when his dad became sick. The high elevations made his dad feel weak and made his head hurt.

SUMMIT 5
Mount McKinley
in North America
20,320 feet

JORDAN'S CLIMB
June 2008, age 11

Climbing this mountain's summit ridge was scary. Jordan had to use the right gear to avoid slipping off the high, snowy ledge.

SUMMIT 7
Vinson Massif
in Antarctica
16,067 feet

JORDAN'S CLIMB
December 2011, age 15

Jordan achieved his Seven Summit goal. He climbed this mountain in the summer. But Jordan and his team still braved very cold temperatures.

breathe. Sometimes higher elevations also cause people to get headaches and stomachaches. This is called elevation sickness. After months of hard work, Jordan was ready to start tackling his goal—climbing the highest mountain on each of the seven continents.

∧ Jordan celebrates a successful climb in New Guinea.

SUMMIT 6
Mount Everest
in Asia
29,023 feet

JORDAN'S CLIMB
May 2010, age 13

Jordan became the youngest person to climb Everest. For weeks, he climbed up and down parts of the mountain to get used to the elevation.

SUMMIT 2
Mount Kosciuszko
(kosh-CHOOSH-ko)
in Australia
7,310 feet

JORDAN'S CLIMB
April 2007, age 10

Jordan thought this climb would be easy because it is a smaller mountain. But cold temperatures, rain, and wind slowed him down.

SUMMIT 1
Mount Kilimanjaro
(kil-uh-muhn-JAHR-oh)
in Africa
19,340 feet

JORDAN'S CLIMB
July 2006, age 10

Jordan traveled through warm rain forests, over hard lava, and even slippery snow and ice to climb "Kili."

BONUS CLIMB
Carstensz Pyramid
(KAR-stunz)
in New Guinea
16,023 feet

JORDAN'S CLIMB
September 2009, age 13

Jordan also climbed Carstensz Pyramid in New Guinea. Some people argue this peak, not Mount Kosciuszko, is part of the Seven Summits.

Jordan's Most Challenging Summit

Mount Everest wasn't Jordan's last climb during his quest to meet his goal, but it was his most challenging climb. Located in Asia, Mount Everest is the highest mountain in the world. Climbers face intense dangers while climbing it, such as freezing temperatures and harsh winds. Deadly avalanches, or large amounts of sliding ice and snow, injure climbers every year.

Jordan was not afraid of these dangers because he was with his trusted team—his dad, Paul, stepmom, Karen, and three guides called *Sherpas*. Sherpas are skilled climbers who live near the mountain. Jordan's team had packed warm clothing and special climbing boots that helped them grip the ice. Hooks, ropes, tools, tents, and oxygen all helped them reach the summit. Still, the journey to the top was exhausting. At times, Jordan's legs felt as heavy as cement.

Jordan kept walking because he was determined to conquer the mountain and get closer to reaching his Seven Summit goal. At the top of the peak, Jordan recalls, "It was the best 20 minutes of my life, seeing the curvature of the Earth and endless miles." However, he couldn't enjoy his achievement for long because it is very cold on top of Mount Everest. Jordan made sure to do one thing before he started climbing back down. He called his mom, Leigh Anne.

"Mom," he said after this special climb, "I'm calling you from the top of the world."

< Jordan (right) and a Sherpa guide wear masks during their climb. The masks help them breathe the thin mountain air.

Yes, that's Jordan buried under all of that warm clothing. It protects him from the weather as he climbs Mount Everest.

Getting to Know Jordan

You could say that for Jordan, every day is an adventure.
He sets big goals and does what it takes to achieve them.
Let's get to know Jordan a little better in this interview.

National Geographic: How did you get interested in mountain climbing?

Jordan Romero: I originally got outdoors to see nature. I really liked animals, especially snakes. Then it was watching films about the big mountain peaks on Discovery Channel and National Geographic that really sparked my interest for climbing.

NG: Did you do anything unusual to train for a big climb?

JR: For some climbs we have to pull sleds full of gear up the mountain. So I tied a tire to my waist and dragged it behind me to practice pulling the weight.

NG: Were you scared while climbing Mount Everest?

JR: On day 17, Dad and I got swept up in an avalanche, and Dad got a bit hurt. It scared me for a day or so, then we got back on-mission.

NG: Did you have to do schoolwork on each of your climbs?

JR: I had to travel with all my studies and books, and I was doing algebra on Mount Everest. It was hard doing homework on climbs, but it had to get done.

NG: How was climbing Mount Everest with your family?

JR: It was the time of my life. They put it all on the line for me. I'm grateful for their support.

NG: What are your current goals?

JR: I'd like to complete the Adventure Grand Slam. This involves climbing the Seven Summits (done!) and trekking to the North and South Poles. My mom and I are also planning to help build a school in Malawi, a country in Africa.

Jordan stays safe by using ropes. He attaches the ropes to himself and to the mountain. They will catch him if he stumbles.

Jordan, 14, leads a blind climber to the summit of Quandary Peak in Colorado.

Check In What mountain do you think was the hardest for Jordan to climb? Why?

Surfing the Snowy Mountains

by Sean O'Shea

A snowboarder spins and swirls over the snow.

Imagine zipping down the side of a snowy mountain. Your boots are clipped to a snowboard, which is like a short, wide ski. You hit a snowdrift that launches you into the air. Fresh snow hits your cheeks. Hold on!

If you've ever surfed a wave on the ocean or landed a trick on a skateboard, you might know what riding the slopes on a snowboard is like. You stand on the board in much the same way. You bend your knees and hold your balance. But instead of being on the water or at the skate park, you're on a snowy slope or hillside.

Some boarders think the most exciting spot to snowboard is in a **bowl**, or curved area of snow, where snowboarders can swoosh back and forth. Think of a big scoop of earth taken out of the ground. Then add snow. With their curved bowls, steep slopes, and thick powdery snow, no wonder mountain communities are an ideal place to snowboard.

How Snowboarding Became a Sport

1963
Seventh grader Tom Sims builds a "ski board." He wants a way to skateboard in the snow.

1970s
Early snowboarders make their own snowboards. Their designs become popular. Several companies begin to make them.

1980s
Snowboarders begin to get together for contests around the world.

1998
Snowboarding becomes a sport in the Winter Olympic Games. The Olympics at Nagano, Japan, are the first to include snowboarding events.

2000
Snowboarding becomes the fastest-growing sport in the United States.

Gearing Up

Snowboarding is a challenging sport. It can also be dangerous. When a snowboarder shreds, or rides on the edges of the board, he or she has to make quick decisions to stay safe—and upright. It takes years of training and hard work to become a snowboarding **athlete**. Here is some of the gear that snowboarders use on the slopes.

Snowboards are five to six feet long. Most snowboards are about ten inches wide. They come in many shapes and sizes. Different snowboards help you do different tricks. They also help you control your speed and make turns.

Boots and bindings attach to your feet. They keep you on the board.

A helmet protects your head. It also keeps your head warm.

Goggles protect your eyes from snow, ice, wind, and sunlight.

Warm jackets and snow pants keep you warm and dry. Snowboarders need to be able to move freely in their clothing.

Gloves with padding protect your hands when you steer. That's important because boarders steer by dragging one hand along the snowy ground.

A leash keeps the board from sliding away if you fall.

Crust-Bustin' Moves

Method Air
Bend your knees during a jump to bring the board behind you while you grab the board with one hand.

McTwist
Twist around twice as you flip in the air. Skateboarder Mike McGill invented this trick. Others have added more moves to the McTwist to make it even harder!

180 Grind
Turn yourself and your snowboard halfway around as you jump onto the rail. Then turn back at the end of the rail, so you finish facing the same side you started. The rail used can be a stairway rail or a small wall made just for snowboarding.

Giants of the Slopes

Shaun White

These snowboarders are just three of the many champions of this extreme sport.

Shaun White's nickname is the "Flying Tomato" thanks to his red hair and his snowboard tricks. Shaun won his first competition at age seven. Since then, he has won two Olympic medals. At the 2010 games, he performed the "double McTwist 1260." In this trick, he flips twice while doing three-and-a-half spins!

> Shaun White catches some air at a competition in Colorado.

Travis Rice

∧ Travis Rice launches off a hill in Colorado.

A Wyoming native, Travis Rice grew up on the slopes. Travis is a snowboard **freestyle** champion. A freestyle snowboarder performs tricks in a ramp shaped like a capital "U" called a half-pipe. His specialty is Big Air, which is what snowboarders call high jumps. You can even see him performing snowboarding stunts in several movies.

Kelly Clark grew up in Vermont near steep, snowy mountains. Vermont is an excellent place for snowboarding. She has won more medals, including two Olympic medals, in snowboarding than any other female athlete. In 2011, she landed three turns in the air, called a 1080, a first for any woman!

⌄ Kelly Clark competes in a half-pipe event in New York State.

Kelly Clark

Check In Describe your favorite snowboarder or snowboarding move.

Comparing
Mountain Communities

by Annaliese Toth

Two Locations

Mountain communities are in every corner of the world. Let's compare two communities in different countries to see how they are alike and different.

CRESTED BUTTE The Rocky Mountains are located in North America. The community of Crested Butte (BEWT), Colorado, is located in a valley in the Rockies. A valley is a low area between mountains. Even though this town is in a valley, its elevation is 8,885 feet above sea level. Crested Butte can get snow as early as September and as late as June. Summer brings temperatures of about 70°F.

KATHMANDU The Himalaya Mountains stretch across South Asia. They include the country of Nepal. Kathmandu (kat-man-DOO) is the capital city of Nepal. It is located in a river valley near the Himalaya. The elevation of Kathmandu is about 4,344 feet above sea level. The lower elevation helps the people of Kathmandu enjoy a mild climate. The average temperature in the summer is 77°F. Winter temperatures usually don't dip below freezing. In fact, snow is rare in the area. Residents usually go several years without getting any snow at all.

Populations

CRESTED BUTTE   Crested Butte is a **rural** community. This small town doesn't even have a traffic light. Many people visit Crested Butte, but its **population**, or the number of people who live there, is only about 1,500. Residents of Crested Butte must go to nearby communities for many of the services they need. The town of Gunnison has the closest airport. Aspen has the closest hospital. Crested Butte is not big enough to have full-time firefighters. Instead, volunteers help fight fires. For many years, students from Crested Butte even traveled to Gunnison to go to high school.

KATHMANDU More than one million people live in Kathmandu. That's over 600 times the population of Crested Butte! It is the largest city in Nepal and the main business center. This city has access to many services that people need. In fact, Kathmandu has several hospitals and schools, which are difficult to find in the rest of the country.

Resources

CRESTED BUTTE Around 1860, settlers from the eastern part of the United States traveled west. They came to mine gold and coal in places such as Crested Butte. As settlers began mining these **resources**, new businesses opened to serve the miners. Crested Butte flourished until the supply of gold and coal ran low. Many mines closed. Some settlers tried to earn money by ranching on the grassland. Others cut down trees and turned them into lumber they could sell. However, people still couldn't earn enough money to support their families. By the 1950s, the population of Crested Butte had gotten smaller because people moved away.

KATHMANDU Resources are also the reason people formed a community in Kathmandu. The valley where this city is located has many rivers running through it. People live here for the plentiful water. Growing crops can be difficult on the steep sides of mountains. But in the valley, the rich soil and good weather allow crops such as wheat to grow easily. The valley has other benefits, too. It gives people a way to pass through the tallest mountains in the world.

Tourism

CRESTED BUTTE In the cool summer weather, the trails that curve throughout the Rockies near Crested Butte are fun to explore by foot or by bike. In the winter, snowboarders spin in the air and skiers weave back and forth down the snowy mountains. Hotels, ski lodges, and restaurants welcome **tourists**, or visitors to the community, all year. Most people who live and work in Crested Butte have jobs helping tourists. Others work in the mountains removing snow from roads and maintaining ski trails or bike paths.

KATHMANDU Kathmandu serves as the starting point for many tourists who are planning to climb in the Himalaya. In 1953, the first climbers reached the summit of nearby Mount Everest, the world's highest mountain. Since then, the people of Kathmandu have opened stores, restaurants, and hotels to serve people who come to visit the mountains. Before the 1950s, there was not a single hotel in Kathmandu.

While there may be differences among them, all mountain communities have at least one thing in common—mountains!

Check In How are Crested Butte and Kathmandu similar?

Discuss

1. What do you think connects the three selections that you read in this book? What makes you think that?

2. If you lived in or visited a mountain community, what kinds of goals could you set for yourself? Why?

3. What kinds of activities can you do to have fun in the mountains?

4. What is similar about the community you live in and mountain communities like Crested Butte and Kathmandu? What is different?

5. What do you still wonder about living in the mountains?